Copyright © 2015 Angela Doll Carlson
All Rights Reserved
ISBN - 978-1518722363
DoxaSoma: The Daily Practice of Advent

Without limiting the rights under copyright reserved above, no part of this publication may be reproduced, stored in or introduced into a retrieval system, or transmitted, in any form, or by any means (electronic, mechanical, photocopying, recording, or otherwise), without the prior written permission of Angela Doll Carlson.

The Daily Practice of Praise

Book Two: Advent

Angela Doll Carlson

Practice-

What do you

practice

in your daily life?

An instrument?

A sport?

A mindset?

What about Grace?

Mercy?

Forgiveness?

Patience?

All disciplines require practice whether they are physical or spiritual. Practice is a way for us to gain skill and understanding in our disciplines. Practice makes us strong. It requires sacrifice. It requires commitment.

DoxaSoma is the integration of our prayer lives with our bodily selves. We align our movements to embody the Word of God. We practice this integration. We breathe the word, the prayer, the moment.

This book is a tool for your practice. It is a way to build this practice of DoxaSoma. It is a way to make room for Holy Spirit just as we make room for the air we breathe.

Book Two in this series focuses on the season of Advent— that period of time which leads us into Christmas— the celebration of the birth of our Savior.

Take a few minutes in each day— a few minutes of quiet for the next 24 days as we enter the season of Advent

to dwell in the anticipation of Christ's birth,

to listen for joy,

to make each breath a prayer.

-Angela Doll Carlson

The Daily Practice

Each day you will learn and practice a new position. Each position will build upon the previous day's work.

We will begin slowly, stretching, understanding our bodies. Pay careful attention during this time.

Work toward shifting, slowly, from the mechanics (*HOW* you move) to the purpose, (*WHY* you move.) In this way we shift from merely "stretching" our muscles to using our bodies as instruments of praise.

Use the reflection questions to bring new insights into your practice. Journal your answers. See what God has for you in this way.

Move FIRST for safety:
Always keep soft joints at the elbows and the knees in particular. Never lock your joints. Stability comes from the entire body, not from the joint alone.

Always hinge at the *hip* first when bending forward. Folding at the waist is acceptable only after you have gone as far as you can go by hinging at the hip.

Breathe freely. Never hold your breath while holding a position. Your breath gives you energy and strength. You need this inflow and outflow for clear movement.

Keep your "core" strong. Your core refers to the band of muscles around your midsection including your abdominals, your glutes, and your lower back. Keep these strong and engaged. They are there to protect you.

Be sure to work both sides of the body evenly. If a position requires balance work the do one side and the opposite side as well.

Pain is your body's way of telling you that something is amiss. If you feel pain, STOP. You should feel the movement of your muscles, the feeling of deep stretching at times and even perhaps some muscle fatigue. This is good. Pain, however, tells you to stop. Please listen to your body. Take it slowly.

At the end of the 14th day and on the 25th day you will cycle through the sequence of movements from the previous days. Take your time.

Choose a verse that spoke to you and breathe that as you move. Choose some music that speaks of praise as you move.

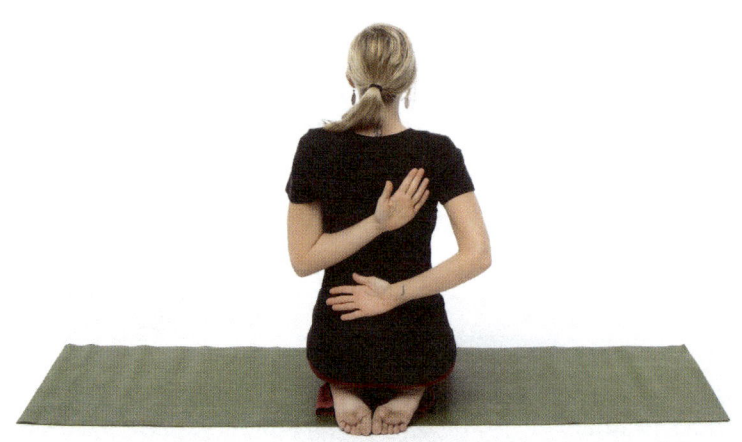

Advent

God With Us

For Christians, Advent is meant to be a time of preparation, of hope, peace and joy. We are most specifically preparing ourselves for Christmas or perhaps more accurately, we are retelling the story of Christ. We are preparing ourselves again for the "coming" of Christ into our midst. It is a sacramental time, a waiting place.

This waiting place has a lot to offer us. The tough thing about Advent is that we wait whether we want to or not. We don't really have a choice in it.

Waiting can be uncomfortable. Advent is simply an awareness that we are, in fact, waiting.

The calendar moves the way it's going to move. The thing that speeds it up is the busy-ness we choose. We find things to fill up that time— to make it pass without pain or discomfort that comes with waiting.

Medicating the waiting time only leads to feeling let down, disappointed and angry when all is said and done. We end up with moments of reflection later that start less often with "wasn't it great when…." and more with "I wish I had…"

This is what we are working to avoid in this mindfulness prayerful practice during Advent. Perhaps that's a good way for us all to move through seasons of waiting, especially this one. Perhaps all waiting has a sacred bent to it, an opportunity to practice something important while we wait, something embracing the mystery and the mundane all at the same time.

Use this time and this book to reach those sacred places, those waiting places— places that are open and ready to receive the gift that is Christ in our midst as we wait in hope.

Day 1

Prayer

"In His hand is the life of every creature and the breath of all mankind." Job 12:10

Prayer position is the way we begin.

By placing our hands at the heart, thumbs together as our palms are pressing in we are reminded to lift up.

We let our hands remind us to be still, to be present, to pay attention to our breathing and to lift at the heart.

By lifting at the heart we put our bodies back into right relationship with our Creator, open and willing and ready. We put our shoulders in alignment with our head and our spine. We are lifting at the heart and finding our starting place in our breath.

Today, on this first day of your Advent practice, spend time just breathing. Think of this time as a way to set the intention for this season. Consider what it is you hope for during this time. Breathe in long, slow and steady breaths. Let the air completely fill your lungs and on the exhale imagine letting go of fear and doubt and the "busyness" the season can often bring. Focus only on the breath, the feel of your palms pressing, thumbs together, here, at the heart. This is where is all begins.

"In His hand is the life of every creature and the breath of all mankind." Job 12:10

For reflection-

As you start your Advent practice consider keeping a prayer journal to keep track of how you felt during the positions, what came to you during prayer and how you can engage this season of waiting to the fullest.

What are your hopes for today? For this week? For this season?

When you breathe in this prayer position today can you set an intention for this Advent season? Is it Peace? Calm? Charity? Choose something you can carry through this next 24 days.

Choose one word or image to anchor this intention today. Perhaps choose a verse to accompany it. Write it down so that you'll remember each day as you breathe and pray. This is where you want to be rooted this holiday season.

Day 2

Dove

O, that I had the wings of a dove!
I would fly away and be at rest."
Psalm 55:6

Every position in DoxaSoma works in conjunction with other positions. We often say that one position asks a question and another will provide the answer. The question asked by hands in Prayer position is answered often by arms moving into what we call "Dove."

Draw the hands forward before you, straightening the arms then widen out the arms to either side of the body. Keep your shoulders away from the ears, pressing the shoulder blades together in back and lifting at the heart again. With the palms facing outward press the arms back further and open at the heart.

This is a vulnerable position, with the heart open like this. As you begin your Advent journey bear in mind those places where you hide. A hunched forward posture is a protected posture and over time it can cause the muscles of the chest to tighten and over-stretching the muscles of the upper back. Use this position to feel that protected posture dissipate. Open up!

"O, that I had the wings of a dove! I would fly away and be at rest." Psalm 55:6

For reflection-

The season of Advent is a time of waiting, gestation, beginning. Consider today what new life is beginning around you. Opening up in Dove is a way to make room for this new life.

What makes you move into "protected" positions throughout your day- on a physical level, an emotional level or a spiritual level?

What keeps you from trusting God with your heart when you take those protected positions? When you breathe and open up in this Dove position today can imagine that God is waiting for this vulnerability?

Choose one word or image to anchor this trust today. Perhaps choose a verse to accompany it.

Day 3

Praise

*"My feet stand on level ground;
in the great congregation
I will praise the Lord."
Psalm 26:12*

After centering and steadying ourselves in Prayer and then opening at the heart with Dove, the best possible destination is the wide embrace of Praise position.

From Dove we raise the arms on either side with palms open and shoulders away from the ears. We keep the arms fairly wide once raised with soft elbows and shoulder blades together and back.

This wide posture for the arms means the lungs have lots of space for deep inhaling followed by full and complete exhaling. We call this "good breathing" in DoxaSoma. Spend a few moments in this good breathing today. Remember your focus for the season as you cycle through Prayer position to Dove to Praise. To complete this arm sequence, draw your palms together above your head and bring your hands back to prayer at the heart. Cycle through this a number of times paying attention to your breathing. This is a good stress reliever and as the materialistic, consumer focused world presses in, this will come in handy.

"My feet stand on level ground; in the great congregation I will praise the Lord."
Psalm 26:12

For reflection- Consider a moment this part of the verse today, "In the great congregation, I will praise the Lord." When the consumer level of the Christmas season kicks up it's hard not to get swept away by it and go along with the shopping crowd. What's at risk for you to move out of that crowd and reassess the reason for the season?

In this position of Praise or with a cycle of Prayer, Dove and Praise, pay attention to what you feel in your body. Can you spot places that are sore or in need of more movement, stretching and strength? Write about what you feel here and how it might connect with the emotional stresses in your life.

It's important in all of these arm positions to keep the hands open, not balled up in a fist. Where else do you need to keep an open position this holiday season?

Day 4

Waiting

*"Blessed are those who listen to me,
watching daily at my doors, waiting at my doorway."
Proverbs 8:34*

Waiting is our watchword for Advent so it's right that we set this intention with this position right at the start of the season. There is much to be gained in waiting.

We can do the first three positions either sitting, kneeling or standing but for Waiting, take a seated position on your mat. Stacking the feet one in front of other or "cross-legged," lift first at the heart to get the body back into right relationship with itself, aligning the spine and neck and engaging the stretch in the back of the leg and deep muscles of the glutes.

While in this position, as you feel the stretch release, walk the fingers or hands forward on the mat, hinging at the hips and lifting the heart and slowly increase the stretch.

When you cannot go any further by hinging, fold at the waist into the full extension of Waiting. Be sure to breathe with each movement, good breathing here! Don't forget to switch your foot position placing the other foot in front and stretch the other side as well to keep it balanced.

"Blessed are those who listen to me, watching daily at my doors, waiting at my doorway."
Proverbs 8:34

For reflection-

If you celebrated Christmas a child you may remember the "waiting" those few weeks until the day arrived. Now, as an adult, can you get in touch with the joyful, childlike anticipation today?

If you have contact with that anticipation spend some time there while sitting in the position of Waiting. Breathe that joy. What does that joy tell you about this season of Advent?

The verse for Waiting speaks of waiting at the doorstep. When you picture this type of waiting, what does it bring to mind for you? Can you see yourself waiting for God at His doorstep, listening for Him?

Day 5

Sacrifice

*"May my prayer be set before you like incense;
may the lifting up of my hands be like the evening sacrifice."*

Psalm 141:2

Times of waiting, even waiting for something hopeful, bring with them a degree of sacrifice. We give up time, or the need to "have it now" in order to reach some higher goal, gain some greater treasure.

From Waiting, draw your legs up toward the body, contract at the abdominals and lift at the heart as you balance. You may lightly hold your knees close to the body in this position or to add intensity you may release the hands, even lifting them up before you as the verse suggests. Remember to keep even breathing here. Remember to keep the abdominals contracted and the heart lifted.

In this position you want to be sure that the head is aligned with the body, floating in a neutral position. You may want to choose a focus point at eye level to help with this and to aid in the balancing as well. Having a steady focus point is an important aspect of balance work and spiritual work as well!

"May my prayer be set before you like incense; may the lifting up of my hands be like the evening sacrifice."
Psalm 141:2

For reflection- In this time of waiting, what is the sacrifice you consider as you spend time in this position?

Sometimes in the busy-ness of the season, we lose track of our focus and it's often our relationships that suffer as a result. Have you experienced this? What kinds of "busy-ness" have you seen cut into your family time? Your relationship building time?

If there were one thing you could (or maybe should) give up for these next few weeks to make room for contemplation and prayer, what would it be? Can you commit to make the sacrifice?

Day 6

Harp

*"Awake, my soul! Awake, harp and lyre!
I will awaken the dawn!"
Psalm 57:8*

We are called to joy. This Advent season has joy knitted within it.

The waiting and the sacrifice can sometimes cause us to forget this call to joy. We get also caught up in the trappings of the season, events that are meant to boost our Christmas joy can often lead to more stress, cutting us off from the real meaning of our celebration of Christmas— the coming of Christ into our world.

From the position of Sacrifice we find our balance, lift at the heart and begin to straighten the legs, keeping the hands placed lightly on the back of the thigh or the calf. Head is in a neutral position by fixing your gaze at about ankle level. Work toward straightening the legs and lifting the heart.

Remember to breath as you extend the legs, keeping the heart lifted and shoulders away from the ears. This position can also be done back lying. This will decrease the intensity on the lower back but may put stress on the neck. Be sure to keep the neck in a neutral position to alleviate this by fixing the gaze a bit higher, lifting the chin.

"Awake, my soul!
Awake, harp and lyre!
I will awaken the dawn!"
Psalm 57:8

For reflection-

In this position pay attention to your breathing, making sure that you maintain your "good breathing" throughout. Pay attention to how that changes the position for you. What do you feel in this position?

When you consider the words in the verse here, "Awake, my soul!" what comes to mind? Are there places in your life where you know that your soul is not awake?

What does it look like to rouse your soul to be "awake" during this time of waiting in hope?

Day 7

Ark

*"Let us go to His dwelling place; let us worship at HIs footstool, saying,
'Arise, Lord, and come to your resting place,
you and the ark of your might.'"
Psalm 132:7-8*

We no longer carry around the Ark of the New Covenant to house God's spirit.

We are now that Ark— the temple of the Holy Spirit.

As you shift from awakening the soul in the position of Harp into the position of Ark, find your balance again, lift at the heart and bend at the knees as you begin to release your hands to either side of the body.

Remember in Ark to keep your head in a neutral position to protect your neck and to contract at the abdominals to keep the body strong and the lower back supported. Imagine "zipping up" your abdominals as you would zip up a pair of jeans. This position will help to build strength in the core to support your entire body throughout your day.

This position can also be done in back lying to support the lower back. Keep the chin lifted to alleviate stress on the neck.

"Let us go to His dwelling place; let us worship at His footstool, saying, 'Arise, Lord, and come to your resting place, you and the ark of your might.'"
Psalm 132:7-8

For reflection-

Consider the idea that within you resides the Spirit of God. What does this bring to mind as you practice the position of Ark?

If there is one thing you can do today to reinforce the value and beauty of this vessel what could it be?

In the verse for this position we hear the words, "Let us go to His dwelling place..." What does this phrase bring up for you as you hold this position?

Can you anchor this today in your journal with an image or a word to carry throughout the day? Throughout the season?

Day 8

Wisdom

"To God belong wisdom and power;

counsel and understanding are His."

Job 12:13

We often say in DoxaSoma when we practice this position that we will "sit" in Wisdom. In this way we remind ourselves that wisdom does come from God, and in His time. We are meant to pursue wisdom and to do so with intention and purpose.

It's possible that at first this may not feel as though it will be hard work, simply "sitting" in Wisdom. The real key is the ongoing pursuit and the attention to keeping the body in right alignment. If we do this we are engaging the core, the heart and the quadriceps in the front of the body while stretching primarily the hamstrings at the same time. The position becomes challenging in this way.

In a seated position, place the legs straight in front of the body while flexing the feet. Lift at the heart and place the hands on either side of the body at the mat. Begin hinging at the hip drawing the heart toward the knee and keeping the head neutral. Drop the hands to the top of the legs and "walk" them down slowly, hinging first at the hip then lifting at the heart to bring the spine into alignment. Breathe here, and move slowly to keep the stretch engaged. To finish the position contract at the abdominals, release the flexed foot and fold at the waist, forehead moving toward the knee. Do not force this. Just breathe into it. Your stretch is wherever you find it.

""To God belong wisdom and power; counsel and understanding are His."
Job 12:13

For reflection-

The key to Wisdom is being consistent and attentive. Where do you see a need for this consistence and attentiveness in your daily life?

How can you begin to pursue moments of being consistent and attentive in this season of waiting?

As you practice the position of Wisdom, consider again the anchor you chose for this season. What comes to you as your breathe in this position?

Day 9

Hill & Valley

"Every valley shall be raised up, every mountain and hill made low."

Isaiah 40:4

Life is unpredictable, especially in holiday seasons. Fluid movement makes it possible to handle whatever comes our way with grace.

The position of Hill & Valley, a moving position, is a good way to engage the muscles and build that fluidity.

Move into a hands and knees position, aligning the hands under the shoulders and the knees under the hips. Inhale and "drop" into the Valley by tilting the pelvis forward to curve the lower back, lift the chin up. Then exhale and "press" up into the Hill, bringing the chin to the chest and rounding out the back, pressing out through the mat.

This position works best when done slowly, taking time to feel the fluid motion and align the breathing. By slowing down breathing, extending the inhale and exhale we give the body time to adapt to the shift. Imagine breathing into the belly while in the Valley and emptying the lungs while in the Hill. Take some time with this position and feel the small changes that come as you practice. This position is great for releasing stress and anxiety.

"Every valley shall be raised up, every mountain and hill made low."
Isaiah 40:4

For reflection-

As you practice this position, focusing on "fluid movement" consider what holds you up in your daily walk, especially this season of Advent. What is it that causes "sticking points" throughout the day?

Are you seeing a common theme as you move more deeply into the Advent season and your daily practice of prayer and movement?

In Hill and Valley we look to the verse to remind us that God is more than capable of leveling the road, making the hills low and valleys raised. Where do you see this leveling needed in your own faith walk?

Day 10

Stone Balance

"You show that you are a letter from Christ, the result of our ministry written not with ink but with the Spirit of the living God, not on tablets of stone but on tablets of human hearts."

2 Corinthians 3:3

We continue to practice this Advent season with the theme of Balance. This position helps to build the core with tremendous results, but it takes focus and drive.

The focus for Stone Balance is in finding just the right positioning of the hands and knees. Begin this position in the modified version and starting in hands and knees with a neutral spine. Hands are placed under the shoulders and knees aligned with the hips. Begin by simply raising the left hand, aligned with the ear, neck in neutral position. Contract the glutes and straighten the right leg, keeping the supporting knee bent on the mat.

Hold here and breathe, three "good" breaths and release and then do the same movement on the opposite side. Remember to contract the abdominals and the glutes, keep good form and steady breathing. When you feel strong enough you may do the full extension of the position, shown below. Take your time; don't rush to the full extension. The movement is still quite effective in the modified position.

"You show that you are a letter from Christ, the result of our ministry written not with ink but with the Spirit of the living God, not on tablets of stone but on tablets of human hearts."
2 Corinthians 3:3

For reflection-

The verse for Stone Balance is a compliment to another position in DoxaSoma, called Stone Table. Both positions remind us that Christ is written on our hearts. When you consider this in Stone Balance what does this bring up for you?

Balance and strength come with time and practice. Is there a place in your life where you feel impatience with your own spiritual, physical or emotional health?

How can you release that impatience today? What can you do to make steps toward that health?

Day 11

Holy Ground

"'Do not come any closer,' God said. 'Take off your sandals, for the place where you are standing is holy ground.'"
Exodus 3:5

The foundational element for the position of Holy Ground is reverence. We take a moment today to stop our work long enough to acknowledge the sacred, to breathe and to give thanks.

From the position of Stone Balance we return to our hands and knees position, take a minute to "reset" ourselves and then lower the forehead toward the mat as though bowing before God.

Breathe through this movement, taking in the reverence of the action and moving slowly. The more slowly we move here, the more time we spend in this, the more in touch we become with witnessing the sacred in our every day lives.

As you press back up into the starting position, take a deep exhale and perhaps pull back into the position of Elijah to rest before moving on. In Elijah we sit back on the heels, forehead to the mat. This is a position of rest and a good place regroup at this midpoint of the season.

"'Do not come any closer,' God said. 'Take off your sandals, for the place where you are standing is holy ground.'"
Exodus 3:5

For reflection- As we move through Holy Ground try to release any stresses or fears as you move the forehead toward the mat. What is it that you must lay aside as you come closer to Christmas?

Pay attention today to seeing the wonder and power of God's work around you. Where do you spot His hand in your daily life?

Take note of those moments that feel sacred today. Write them down in your journal. How can you hold on to those moments when things are busy?

Day 12

Stone Table

"You also, like living stones, are being built into a spiritual house to be a holy priesthood, offering spiritual sacrifices acceptable to God through Jesus Christ."
1 Peter 2:5

Without a strong core, we are an injury waiting to happen. In the practice of DoxaSoma we correlate the "core" of the body with support and in our faith lives, this is best evidenced in our community. This is where we draw our support.

Just as Stone Table anchors us in our DoxaSoma practice and builds the support we need for a strong practice, our faith communities anchor us in this season of Advent. When the holidays kick up into high gear this next few weeks, our faith communities can remind us where we are rooted and help to remind us of our focus.

From Holy Ground or a hands and knees position, align body weight over the hands and straighten the legs. Press the shoulder blades together and keep the body in alignment by contracting at the core and keeping head in a neutral position. To decrease the intensity you can drop the knees to the mat but keep the body weight over the hands as in a modified push up position.

Breath in this position and hold for a count of at least three breaths, working to extend the inhale and exhale as you keep good form.

"You also, like living stones, are being built into a spiritual house to be a holy priesthood, offering spiritual sacrifices acceptable to God through Jesus Christ."
1 Peter 2:5

For reflection- As you hold Stone Table consider your own support community. Consider how they help to build you up in your spiritual journey. Write about this today in your journal.

While in this position, notice how small adjustments change the position for you. Where do you feel this in your body? What feels like the "anchor" in this position?

How are you anchored this holiday season as you wait? Breathe this anchor while holding Stone Table.

Take this opportunity to link the positions for the first half of this season and create a "Doxa" or Praise sequence. Spend some time in each position, not rushing to move from one to another. Remember to keep your breathing even and your movement fluid. Begin in a seated position.

Positions: Days 1-12

Hands together at the heart, breathing is steady and even.

Dove Position: Heart open and lifted, palms facing out.

Praise Position: Arms lifted, shoulders down

Waiting: Legs stacked, heart lifted, palms walking forward

Ark Position: Balanced on sitz bones, knees bent and heart lifted

Wisdom: Legs straight and heart lifted, hands walking forward

Sacrifice: Balance on sitz bones, knees drawn in, heart lifted

Harp: heart lifted and legs extended

Hill: Back rounded, chin to chest, pressing out through hands

Valley: Pelvis tipped forward, lower back curved, chin lifted

Stone Balance: Alternate arm and leg lifted, head aligned with arm

Holy Ground: Forehead to mat, breathing steady

Stone Table: body straight, pressing out through hands, head aligned with body

Day 13

Tent

*"I long to dwell in your tent forever
and take refuge in the shelter of your wings."
Psalm 61:4*

The response to the external pressure of the season can lead some people to withdraw, to hide and just wait it out. The impulse to pull in is not a bad one but the motivation, especially during Advent is important to note.

The weeks leading up to the celebration of Christmas can become filled with commitments, parties, shopping, cooking and family visits. The position of Tent here can offer a safe place, not to hide out— but to find some rest in the midst of it all.

Tent is a complimentary position to Stone Table meaning that after the core work in Stone Table the shift to Tent engages another set of muscles. The movement between the two then feels like a relief, a safe place to find some rest.

From Stone Table, contract at the abdominals and press hips up into Tent, keeping the knees and elbows flexible, not locked and aligning the head with the arms. Work toward flattening the feet over time. Remember to take advantage of this "rest" with a deep inhale and full exhale.

"I long to dwell in your tent forever and take refuge in the shelter of your wings."
Psalm 61:4

For reflection-

As you breathe in this position consider the anchor you found at the start of the season and the anchoring you felt in Stone Table. Do these feel connected?

What places do you see yourself needing shelter this month, this season? What does that shelter look like to you?

As you practice Tent, move between Stone Table and Tent to feel that fluid motion and imagine that this is the move from the external pressure of the season into that safe dwelling place offered by God. What does this feel like to you knowing you have that safe place?

For the next position you'll transition to standing from Tent position by dropping the knees to the mat, rolling up onto the ball of the foot and finding your balance. Then bend at the knees and hinge up to standing.

Day 14

Throne

*Let us then approach God's throne of grace with confidence,
so that we may receive mercy and find grace
to help us in our time of need."
Hebrews 4:16*

As we move closer to Christmas this is a good time to remind ourselves that we are making ready. We are approaching the joyful event with great anticipation but we are not there yet. There is still work to be done, not the shopping and cooking and wrapping but the preparation of our hearts. We are making ready. Today as you work in this position let this be your guiding focus.

From the Standing position bring hands to the heart in Prayer and hinge at the hip to a bow. Bend at the knees as though you are sitting down into a chair. Keep the knees behind the toes and lower back flat, contracting the abdominals and lifting at the heart. To intensify this position sit further down into it but keep the knees behind the toes and continue to lift at the heart as much as you are able.

Breathe with intention and focus, in through the nose and out through pursed lips. Hold for at least three good breaths or until fatigued. The longer this position is held, the more strength will be built.

"Let us then approach God's throne of grace with confidence, so that we may receive mercy and find grace to help us in our time of need." Hebrews 4:16

For reflection-

Your focus for today is about preparation, making ready. What is it that comes to mind for you around this as you hold Throne and breathe?

Our verse for this position speaks of approaching God's throne with confidence. Can you get in touch with this confidence today? Where do you see this in your everyday life?

How can this confidence help you to pursue God's presence in this season?

Day 15

Authority

"I have given you authority to trample on snakes and scorpions and to overcome all the power of the enemy; nothing will harm you."
Luke 10:19

Being or having authority brings with it a great deal of responsibility. Often that responsibility can be a heavy weight that we carry around. If we fail to see the gift we have been given in this it's easy to become resentful and want to retreat. During this season of Advent we may find ourselves buried under the responsibilities of our roles, as spouse or parent, sibling or friend. On this day take a moment to breathe and remember that the authority you hold gives you strength in this time of waiting. Feel the strength of the authority you've been given to overcome the evil that presses in from all sides.

From Throne, lift up, hands to heart and bringing one leg forward. Straighten that leg, flexing the foot and sit back down into the position as you bring your arms out before you, hands into fists.

To intensify this position, deepen on the bent leg but take care not to let the knee move past the toe. Hold and breathe through this position with steady even breaths.

"I have given you authority to trample on snakes and scorpions and to overcome all the power of the enemy; nothing will harm you."
Luke 10:19

For reflection-

In the position of Authority consider where you see God's strength in your life. Where do you see His hand?

What does the verse bring up for you in this season of Advent? Do you see any places in which you've had to step into a place of authority in this time?

What does it look like to step into that authority and still remain vulnerable to God?

Day 16

Rejoice

*Rejoice in the Lord always.
I will say it again, Rejoice!
"Phillippians 4:4*

As the time grows closer to the celebration of God's becoming man and dwelling among us we are likely to be hit with our "to do" list full in the face. Just at the moment we are primed to get in touch with the rejoicing we are at our most vulnerable time-wise.

The position of Rejoice is a beautiful release from the strong and deep position of Authority. Where Authority builds strength by standing firm, Rejoice opens us up with fluid motion, completing the picture in the sequence of movements.

From Authority, shift the body weight by stepping forward into the front leg while straightening the back leg and lifting. Arms raise forward, palms open and heart lifted. Remember to contract at the glutes and point the toe to keep that back leg energized.

Keep shoulders away from ears with the raised arms position and keep the standing leg soft at the knee, never locked. Breathe here, keeping the breath even and full. To add intensity tilt the body forward and lift the back leg a bit higher. Remember to contract at the abdominals as well to support the core.

For reflection-

The verse for this position reminds us that we are to "rejoice" in the Lord and in fact, it repeats this command immediately for added emphasis. When you think of rejoicing in the Lord "always" what comes to mind for you?

Take time to test out the sequence of movement from Authority to Rejoice. What comes to you in that small cycle of movement? Can you connect those two movements with how you're feeling in this time of waiting?

While holding the leg position for Rejoice, take a few moments to shift the arm position, drawing the hands to the heart and cycling through Prayer Breathing. Can you get in touch with the feeling of rejoicing?

Day 17

Standing Dove

*"Oh that I had the wings of a dove!
I would fly away and be at rest."
Psalm 55:6*

The signs that are blinking on our computer screens, the ads in the Sunday paper or on the billboards along the road tell us that there are only x number of shopping days until Christmas. The countdown in on and you are running out of time!

The urge to sprout wings and fly away is strong but fear not! We do not have to be subject to that way of understanding Christmas. We are in the position of being ready and willing to accept the Son of God into the world. We are making ready.

From the position of Rejoice, keeping the standing leg soft at the knee, not locked, tilt the body forward and lift at the heart. Keep the back leg lifted and intensify this lift by contracting the glutes. Open the arms to the "dove" position, focusing on opening and lifting the "heart."

Breathe in this position and the freedom and openness of it. Keep the back leg engaged and foot pointed. Keep your breathing even and steady, paying special attention to lengthening your inhale and exhale to slow down and be fully present.

"Oh that I had the wings of a dove! I would fly away and be at rest."
Psalm 55:6

For reflection-

The hand position for Standing Dove has palms open and outward facing. Consider how this mirrors the posture you are taking in today toward the world. How can you be open today?

As you hold the position and breathe, pay attention to what comes to you. What do you feel in this position? Do you know how you are being stretched? Do you see how you are gaining strength?

Cycle through the three movements of Authority to Rejoice to Standing Dove and then back to Standing then do the same sequence of movements on the other side of the body as well. What do you feel as you breathe the verse through this small series of movements? Do you feel the freedom and strength in it?

Day 18

Eagle's Wings

*"But those who hope in the Lord will renew their strength.
They will soar on wings like eagles; they will run and not grow weary,
they will walk and not be faint."*
Isaiah 40:31

As we practice day after day, we do begin to see changes- strength building, flexibility increasing, stress ebbing away. Eagle's Wings is a position that works against gravity, much like the approach we're taking in this lead up to Christmas. The pull toward consumerism and stress is strong. We have to balance ourselves and keep our focus, build our core, to proceed with grace.

From the position of Standing Dove find your balance, keeping the standing leg slightly bent at the knee so that the knee is not locked. Arms come to either the heart in prayer or to Hope (as pictured below). Raise the back leg and tilt the torso forward keeping the heart open. Contract at the glutes to keep the leg lifted and work toward keeping a straight body position. Head is in a neutral position, aligned with the body. Keep your gaze focused on one point to aid in the balance on this position.

To add intensity vary the arms from Prayer position to Hope being careful not to lose your good form. With each return to Prayer position reset your form, breathing steadily and deeply. Be sure to work each side.

"But those who hope in the Lord will renew their strength. They will soar on wings like eagles; they will run and not grow weary, they will walk and not be faint."
Isaiah 40:31

For reflection-

Balance is the key to approaching this season with the best focus. When you consider "balance" where do you see this lacking in your life this season?

What can you do to bring balance back to your day, your week, this season?

Contemplate these words from the verse today as you work through Eagle's Wings, "They will soar on wings like eagles; they will run and not grow weary." What does this verse bring up for you?

Day 19

Everlasting

*"Before the mountains were born
or you brought forth the whole world,
from everlasting to everlasting you are God."
Psalm 92:2*

In this last week before the celebration of Jesus' birth we are reminded that God is everlasting. Before anything, everything, He was present. His entrance into our world, becoming human, becoming vulnerable, shows his compassion for us, his desire to be in relationship with us. The position of Everlasting is a way for us to get in touch with the reality of this, with the awesome Creator who longs to be in relationship.

From Eagle's Wings, find your balance while straightening the standing leg, Contract at the abdominals and the glutes as you lift the back leg even with the body and draw the arms to either side of the head reaching straight ahead making the body into one continuous line. Keep the ears aligned with the arms to maintain the proper neck position, press out through the whole of the foot and point the toe of the lifted leg.

Breathe evenly here. It's important to remember to direct your breathing even during difficult positions. If needed, use a chair for light support by placing it near the fingers. Touch the back of the chair lightly to maintain balance.

"Before the mountains were born or you brought forth the whole world, from everlasting to everlasting you are God."
Psalm 92:2

For reflection-

So much of our experience here on earth can feel temporary or even mundane. During this wait for Christmas we become aware of the eternal, the everlasting. What can you point to as everlasting or eternal in this season?

As you work in the position of Everlasting, which can be a challenging position, take note of how you are feeling throughout. Can you pay attention during the hard work of balance and strength building to find the deeper implications of this position?

Choose one focus today to carry you through, whether it is the power of the verse for this position, the anchor you set for the season at the start of this journey or another word, phrase or image. Choose something that you can bring to mind today to remember this everlasting quality of God.

Day 20

Standing Cross

*"Whoever wants to be my disciple must deny themselves
and take up their cross and follow me."
Matthew 16:24*

We don't often connect Easter with Christmas. There's simply too much merry making at hand. This is a time for joy and for peace though as Christians we know that is to come. In this time of preparation for new life it's easy to forget that what makes all of this cause for celebration is the sacrifice Christ made for us on the cross. Even in that realization, there is cause for celebration. He came to dwell among us and to sacrifice himself for us.

From the position of Everlasting bring hands to Prayer Position at the heart and lower the leg to return to our standing position. Find your balance setting your gaze straight ahead and draw the leg forward bending at the knee, contracting at the abdominals to engage the core. When your balance is set, bring hands to Christ position, palms facing outward and heart lifted. Be sure to keep your standing leg flexible, not locked at the knee. Breathe evenly here and continue to lift at the knee and the heart to maintain the position.

To intensify this position cycle the hands through Prayer Breathing, being certain to "reset" form at the start of each cycle with hands at the heart.

"Whoever wants to be my disciple must deny themselves and take up their cross and follow me."
Matthew 16:24

For reflection-

As you practice Standing Cross, consider the sacrifice of Christ. What comes to you around this?

If could find a connection between how you approach Christmas in this season of Advent and how you approach Easter in the season of Lent, what would it be?

Even in times of waiting for a joyful event there are moments of fear. Can you identify what fear you carry in this season? Can you be willing to set it aside and trust in God?

Day 21

Prayer Balance

*And when you stand praying,
if you hold anything against anyone, forgive him,
so that your Father in heaven may forgive your sins."
Mark 11:25*

We've already recognized that balance is the key to navigating this Advent season with all the distractions and blinking lights all clamoring for our attention. This position of Prayer Balance continues our work in this area of balance. We find that after several positions- Rejoice, Standing Dove, Eagle's Wings, Everlasting and Standing Cross we begin to experience fatigue. This close to Christmas, this can echo our feelings for the season. Use Prayer Balance to rediscover some energy for Advent.

From Standing Cross, bring hands back to Prayer Position and draw the leg out to the side, pointing the toe. Remember to keep the standing leg soft at the knee, not locked. Lift at the heart.

To modify— keep the toe touching the floor. To intensify— lift from the floor and then cycle the hands through Prayer Breathing.

"And when you stand praying, if you hold anything against anyone, forgive him, so that your Father in heaven may forgive your sins."
Mark 11:25

For reflection-

Get in touch with the fatigue you may feel for the season. Picture where you feel this in your body and breathe into that place while holding the position of Prayer Balance. Can you set that aside for the remainder of this season?

Prayer Balance is another method to move toward "praying without ceasing." In this position pay attention to what your prayer might be as you breathe. What (or who) comes to mind when you stand praying?

We do build up resentments in our daily life. If there were someone you would need to forgive or ask forgiveness of, who would that be? Can you let go of any resentment today as you stand praying?

Day 22

Bowing

*Come, let us bow down in worship,
let us kneel before the Lord our Maker"
Psalm 95:6*

After balance work, Bowing becomes a kind of resting place for us. We are able to stretch those muscles we've been working, sinking into the deep stretch and breathing more deeply. We are coming close to the celebration of Christmas; this is a good place to find rest this week.

From Prayer Balance we return to Standing Prayer, both feet firmly on the mat, knees soft and not locked, hands in prayer position and heart lifted. Before moving into the Bowing position take a moment here to breathe and get accustomed to the feeling of both feet flat on the mat again.

Begin the Bowing by hinging at the hips, heart moving toward the floor but let the hands at Prayer position remind you to keep the heart lifted and shoulder blades together and back. It is a simple movement but form is still very important.

Intensify this position by continuing to hinge forward while keeping the abdominals engaged and heart open. You may fold into a complete Bow after hinging by contracting at the abdominals and folding at the waist, forehead moving toward the knees. Do not force the position.

"Come, let us bow down in worship, let us kneel before the Lord our Maker"
Psalm 95:6

For reflection-

The position of Bowing offers a good solid stretch for the hamstrings and calf muscles in the back of the leg and then in a full fold Bow, a nice release for the lower back. As you breathe into these stretches what comes to you today?

The essence of this practice is worship. As you move through Bowing can you get in touch with the practice of worship?

Bowing is a position of prayer and supplication, laying down our fears and doubts as we come before God in this humble posture. What is it that you need to lay down before God today as we move nearer to Christ's birth?

Day 23

Kneeling Prayer

*When Solomon had finished all these prayers and supplications
to the Lord, he rose from before the altar of the Lord,
where he had been kneeling
with his hands spread out toward heaven."
1 Kings 8:54*

We come to the final days in this time of waiting by transitioning to a kneeling position, Kneeling Prayer. This closes out the sequence of movements and puts us into a position of humility and hope.

From Bowing we move into the full Bow by contracting at the abdominals and folding at the waist while bending the knees. Bend enough so that you can reach the mat with your hands, shifting your body weight to your hands and dropping the knees to the mat.

Once kneeling, bring your hands into prayer position at the heart and lift at the heart. Press the hips forward slightly to keep the spine aligned and begin to center your breathing. This is a cool down position, a good place to ponder this time of waiting in hope. Pay special attention to your breathing and keep your anchor focus as you expand your inhale and exhale.

When Solomon had finished all these prayers and supplications to the Lord, he rose from before the altar of the Lord, where he had been kneeling with his hands spread out toward heaven."
1 Kings 8:54

For reflection-

What comes to you as you practice the position of Kneeling Prayer? Can you focus your breathing and direct your thoughts to prayer here?

The verse for this position speaks of Solomon kneeling before the altar of God. As you practice, try to imagine you are kneeling before the altar of God. What do you bring to the altar in these last few days before Christmas?

Consider your "anchor" for this season. How does it fit with this position of Kneeling Prayer? As you hold and breathe in this position can you connect your anchor?

Day 24

Prayer Breathing

*"Love the Lord your God
with all your heart
and with all your soul
and with all your mind
and with all your strength."
Mark 12:30*

We finish this sequence of movements with the addition of Prayer Breathing to remind us that this season of waiting is an act of love and worship. To keep the focus right during the season of Advent is a way for us as Christians to keep this holiday sacred and set aside. We will still celebrate and participate in the trappings of the culture— the parties, the presents and the stresses— but at the heart of it all is the idea that we are seeking to love God.

In the Kneeling Prayer position with hands beginning in the Prayer position at the heart, inhale bringing the hands to the lips, the forehead and then open and lifted above the head, then circle around on the exhale and move through the movements again. Take your time with this position, extending your breathing and connecting with the verse as you move through it. We often attach the phrase, "In our hearts, in our words and in our thoughts, in these things we praise you, Lord!"

Move through this at least three times to complete the sequence of movements for this Advent season.

"Love the Lord your God with all your heart and with all your soul and with all your mind and with all your strength."
Mark 12:30

For reflection-

One this day before the celebration of Christmas, what stands out to you most profoundly in your practice of DoxaSoma over the course of the season?

How has your anchor helped to keep your focus right?

As you breathe through this series of movements in Prayer Breathing consider that with each breath you are making room for the gift that comes in Christ's birth. What comes to you as you consider this?

Day 25

Doxa

On this Christmas Day you may move through the full sequence of movements for the Advent season. Choose some music to play to help set the right mood for this joyous celebration. Move slowly through the positions one at a time, breathing through it and then fluidly changing to the next position. Run through the sequence doing one side of the body and then once finished start again on the other side of the body to keep the work balanced. Make contact with the joy of this day and begin to shift from the "how" of the positions and into "why" we practice DoxaSoma, to praise and worship God.

Advent Sequence: Days 1-24

Beginning with hands in Prayer Position, heart lifted

Move into Dove position, heart open and lifted

Arms move to Praise, shoulders away from ears

Seated on the mat, stack feet and lift heart for Waiting

Walking hands forward, lifting at heart

Draw legs up to body, balance and lift heart for Sacrifice

Straighten legs, keeping head aligned for Harp

Bend at the knees, lift heart for Ark

Release legs to the mat, lift at the heart and hinge forward for Wisdom

Move to hands and knees for Hill and Valley

dropping the pelvis forward to complete the movement

Straighten the legs and press into Stone Table

Lift at the hips, ears aligned with arms for Tent

Roll to standing and sit into Throne

Bring one leg forward, heel to mat and foot flexed for Authority

Stepping forward, arms lifted for Rejoice

Arms come back, heart open for Standing Dove

Shift body weight and tilt into Eagle's Wings

Draw arms forward for Everlasting

Releasing forward for Standing Cross

Leg sweeps to the side for Standing Prayer Balance

Hinge at the hips for Bowing

From full folded Bow, hands to mat, drop knees for Kneeling Prayer

Hands in Prayer Position to start Prayer Breathing

Hands to lips

Hands to Forehead

Open at the top for Praise

*For to us a child is born,
to us a son is given,
and the government
will be on his shoulders.
And he will be called
Wonderful Counselor,
Mighty God,
Everlasting Father,
Prince of Peace.
Of the greatness of
his government
and peace
there will be no end.*

Isaiah 9: 6-7

Made in the USA
Lexington, KY
19 November 2015